A MAN LIKE MOSES
WALKING IN THE PATH OF JOSEPH

Carlton Matthew White, Sr.

Christine Swain White

A MAN LIKE MOSES
WALKING IN THE PATH OF JOSEPH

Carlton Matthew White, Sr.

Christine Swain White

Copyright © 2020 by Carlton Matthew White, Sr. and
Christine Swain White

All rights reserved. This book or any portion thereof may not be
reproduced or used in any manner whatsoever without the express
written permission of the author except for the use of brief
quotations in a book review or scholarly journal.

Scripture References are taken from the Holy Bible.

Books may be ordered through booksellers.

First Printing: 2020

ISBN 978-0-9998133-7-9

Library of Congress Control Number: 2020909028

NuVision Publishing
PO Box 4455 | Wilmington, NC 28406
www.nuvisiondesigns.biz/publications

Printed in the United States of America.

TABLE OF CONTENTS

Preface 7

Introduction 11

Chapter 1: God's Plan 13

Chapter 2: Paths Of Uncertainties 19

Chapter 4: The Move To New York City 25

Chapter 5: Back Down South 27

Chapter 6: Life Happens 29

Chapter 7: Twist Of Fate 31

Chapter 8: A Word Of Encouragement 33

Chapter 9: The Day The Sun Stopped Shining 35

Chapter 10: God Why? 37

Chapter 11: Favor Behind The Prison Walls 39

Chapter 12: Released From Prison To Home 43

Chapter 13: More Winding Roads 45

Chapter 14: Divine Destiny 47

Chapter 15: The Power To Forgive 51

Epilogue 53

Preface

Everyone has a story to tell. It doesn't matter what nation, town, city or country. Everyone has a story to tell. It doesn't matter whether you are rich or poor, young or old. No matter the race. Everyone has a story to tell. Stories have been written, told and passed along starting from the beginning of time. Some had truth, many had untruth and others had a little of both. Numerous stories that were told have been looked upon as fairy tales or old folk tales but none-the-less, telling stories was a form of entertainment for many grownups and exciting story times for countless children who dared not to go to bed without hearing one or two of the stories. Jesus, even in the bible days, told stories or parables that had powerful meanings to the by standers. These stories were told to the hearers to help them better understand life and its many wonders. I have come to enjoy a good story or two myself and I'm sure many of you have too.

I have a story to tell that will surely touch every heart who reads it. This is a true story about a young man whose life had many twists and turns, ups and downs. But through it all and especially with the help of the Lord, he turned out alright. In this story you will see how life has a way of throwing us many curve balls that we never expected to fly our way. Many of those curve balls were life threatening, but as always, the hands of God showed up right on time and stopped those curve balls right in their tracks. Every time!

One day, after meeting this young man, and after spending some quality time with him, I realized that he had a lot to share. Yes, he had a story to tell. Well, after hearing about all of the many complex things that this young man had been through, it touched my life in such a profound way. It inspired me to share with the whole world what I had been told about this man's life and the many tests and trials that he had to endure. Mind you during this season of the many tests and trials that this young man had to endure, he, like most of us, didn't see the good in it at the moment. It would take years before he finally understood that his life was not just some mistake nor was it just some twist of fate. His life was chosen by the hands of God to endure these tests and trials. Even though he did not understand it back then, he had now come to appreciate the fact that he had to walk this path.

By the time I finished spending days, weeks, months, even years hearing this man life's story, I found myself caught up in his world and it changed my life forever. I then knew that I had to write about this man with all of my heart so that others who may be going through what he had gone through or perhaps others who will go through what this man had been through, would have hope by hearing his story. What is life in this world without hope? After hearing this man's story, I thought about what I should name this book that I would write on this man's behalf. After thinking it over, one special day the Lord dropped this title in my heart. I knew this was the right title because it fit this man's life to the "T".

This book ***"A Man like Moses Walking in the Path of Joseph"*** is a book of hope for those who have traveled paths of uncertainties, despair and darkness, and who have asked this question many times over and over: Why? Why me Lord? With this book, they can now lay their many worries aside. This book will surely bring hope, peace and light to many unanswered questions to the hurting. You, who are holding this very book in your hands, may have been feeling for so long that you needed answers about the many winding roads that you have had to travel. Too many of you have been bound up in your mind thinking that you are a misfit or a mistake. But I assure you that by the time you finish reading this book, you will be set free in your mind, body and soul and you will then understand that no matter what harm may have been planned against you or no matter what ditches may have been dug to trap you, God was, God is and God always will be in charge of your life. And he does indeed have the last say.

Introduction

Many years ago, I met a man who just by looking at him, seemed like just any other ordinary man that I have met lots of times in this life. But one day as I got to know him a little better and especially as we began to communicate more, I realized that this was not just some anybody, but this person was special and unique. We often found ourselves together talking more and more about life and the surprises that it can spring upon us as humans. I heard extraordinary stories about his life from his birth to adulthood. It was something about his stories that reminded me of two other stories that I have heard about and read about in the Bible. Particularly, Bible stories about Moses and Joseph. This is why I decided to write this book. I wanted you to get a chance to read about this man and his life's story so that you could see the similarities between the two bible stories and his life's story.

Take hope in knowing that we are not just born as misfits or mistakes, but we are born for something much greater. We were born with a purpose that is far beyond our own knowledge. This is why it is so important to know God and his holy word, the Bible. It has many spiritual stories that will help us to understand our very existence. A better understanding of our own existence will help us to fully accept how well put together we are according to Psalm

139:14 which says *"I praise you because I am fearfully and wonderfully made; your works are wonderful, I know that full well."* May the wisdom and lessons that you learn from this book bring much encouragement and strength to you as you travel life's winding roads.

Ladies and Gentlemen take a seat and enjoy as I tell the story of **"A Man like Moses Walking in the Path of Joseph"**.

Chapter 1: God's Plan

A long time ago, there was a lady that had many children. One day the lady with the many children had a sister that came to visit her. The lady's sister noticed that there was a baby boy lying on the bed drinking only water from his bottle. The lady's sister saw this and had compassion on him and asked her could she take him home with her for a while. She then suggested that when he is older, she would bring him back. As the story was told to me, the lady's sister, which turned out to be the baby's aunt, never brought him back to his mother. We don't know whether or not there was an agreement for this or not. As time passed, the baby was loved deeply by his aunt and she took good care of him. Each day she loved on him, prayed with him and treasured him as her very on.

In case you didn't catch it, the lady with the many children was the mom of the man who told me about his life's story. Even though the lady that raised him to be a man was his aunt, he called her mom, because she was the only mom that he knew.

As time passed, this little baby began to grow and blossom into a handsome little toddler. While in church with his aunt, she would hold him on her knee while she sang, clapped her hands or read the Bible. The aunt would oftentimes speak life, healing and positive things into his life. She recognized from the first day that she laid her eyes on him that he was a special child. By being a special woman of God herself, she knew in her heart and spirit that she was destined to take the child as her very own.

You see, just like in the Bible story in the book of Exodus when Moses was put in a basket by his mom hoping to keep him from harm, she saw greatness on this child. Also, she loved God and she would not dare let the wicked hands of Pharaoh prematurely end the life of her child. Let's look at how the story progressed.

According to scripture, the story of Moses starts in Exodus Chapter 2:1-10 (NIV). Pharaoh of Egypt had ordered to destroy all of the newborn Hebrew babies by drowning them. But after Moses' mother, Jochebed, gave birth, she made a decision to hide her son.

As Moses began to grow, his mother could no longer hide him, so she had to make a quick and intelligent decision to protect him from Pharaoh. One day she decides to place him in a waterproof bamboo basket in a premeditated spot in the reeds that grew along the side of the Nile River. Moses' mom prayed that someone would find him and take him as their own. It was nothing but the plan of God that had Moses' sister, Miriam, to hide nearby to see what was to happen to her brother Moses. As the baby began to cry, it drew the attention of Pharaoh's daughter who takes the baby from the water. Moses' sister saw that it was safe for her to come out of hiding. As she moved in the spirit of wisdom, she asks the princess if she would like a Hebrew midwife. When the princess agrees,

Miriam moves quickly making sure that Moses' real mother would be the midwife to get paid and to nurse her own child, who now lives in Pharaoh's palace.

You see when God is in the midst, all things will always work out for the good concerning our lives. Just like with the lady in the beginning of the story that had so many children that her sister offered to take one and raise him as her own. As you continue to read the story, you will see that this was God's plan all along. To protect her name, I will call the real mother of the baby boy, "Shining Star". Shining Star's sister's name is Doris (which means "gift") and the baby's name is Carlton. As time went on baby Carlton grew more and more and Doris whom he called mom loved and admired him more and more each day. He was her only boy, so she spoiled him immensely. By the time Carlton grew older he began to participate in the church with Doris. She discovered that he could not only sing but that he loved to sing. The church recognized that he was a gifted child and began to ask him to do small speeches to represent their church. But during this time, even though Carlton enjoyed singing, he was a little afraid to speak because he realized that he had a stuttering problem. Doris realized that he had trouble speaking clearly and she would encourage him to take his time and keep trying.

SPEAKING OF STUTTERING: Did you know that Moses from the Bible had a stuttering problem? Let's look at the scriptures, Exodus 4:10-16 (NIV). *"Moses said to the Lord, 'Pardon your servant, Lord. I have never been eloquent, neither in the past nor since you have spoken to your servant. I am slow of speech and tongue.'"* The Lord said to him, *"Who gave human beings their mouths? Who makes them deaf or mute? Who gives them sight or makes them blind? Is it not I, the Lord? Now go; I will help you speak and will teach you what to say."* But Moses said, *"Pardon your servant, Lord. Please send someone else."* Then the Lord's anger burned against Moses and he said, *"What about your brother, Aaron the Levite? I know he can speak well. He is already on his way to meet you, and he will be glad to see you. You shall speak to him and put words in his mouth; I will help both of you speak and will teach you what to do. He will speak to the people for you, and it will be as if he were your mouth and as if you were God to him."*

We can see here in the Bible story about Moses that even though he grew up in Pharaoh's house of royalty, he still had fears and a low self-esteem about himself because of his speech problem. Carlton was the same way. Even though Doris brought him up in a loving, caring, spiritual home, trained and dressed him well, his speech problem oftentimes would keep him in a state of shame and fear. The other little boys were jealous of him. He feared being mocked and laughed at by them who would tease him for the fun of it.

One thing that I have noticed about life, God has planned our lives out in such a way that no matter how painful situations may seem at times, they are always working for our good. I didn't say that it would always feel good or look good to us, but it will in time work for our good. In the book of Proverbs 16:9 (NIV) it says this: *"In their hearts humans plan their course, but the Lord establishes their steps."* You see this is why it is so very important for us to talk to God about whatever may be on our heart concerning our heart's desires or concerning our everyday business. He already knows what is best for us. It is ok for us to plan but we can rest assure too, that God will order our steps based on what is in His will, for His glory, for our safety and for our good.

When we look through fleshly eyes at the world in which we live, it may seem as if we are in for destruction. But according to the Bible, we, who are on the Lord's side are moving closer and closer to a better day where there will be no more tears, dying, rejection, being talked about, being forsaken etc. Remember, Moses probably felt like an outcast whenever he was mocked among the Egyptian's boys who had better speech than he had. Carlton, according to what he shared with me did feel the same way many times over.

Chapter 2: Paths of Uncertainties

Do you know that God's plans never look like anything that we may plan or have expected in this life? Oftentimes, God's plans look just the opposite of what we may have had in mind. Let's go back to the Bible and take a look at Moses' life. Moses grew big and strong in the Pharaoh's house which had become his home. He had the best teaching and training that any child could have gotten while living in the king's house. I'm sure that Moses felt that his life was on top of the world many days. But one day something happened, and Moses' life was changed forever. Yes, life took a strange twist for him and his paths didn't seem too certain anymore.

Let's look at Exodus 2:11-15 (NIV) *"And it came to pass in those days, when Moses was grown, that he went out unto his brethren, and looked on their burdens: and he spied an Egyptian smiting a Hebrew, one of his brethren. And he looked this way and that way, and when he saw that there was no man, he slew the Egyptian, and hid him in the sand. And when he went out the second day, behold, two men of the Hebrews strove together: and he said to him that did the wrong, wherefore smites thou thy fellow? And he said, who made thee a prince and a judge over us? Intends thou to kill me, as thou killed the Egyptian? And Moses feared, and said, surely this thing is known. Now when Pharaoh heard this thing, he sought to slay Moses. But Moses fled from the face of Pharaoh, and dwelt in the land of Midian: and he sat down by a well."*

See, even though Moses grew up in Pharaoh's home, he knew that he was different and I'm sure oftentimes he felt out of place. And as you just read in the Bible story, he was outside checking on his brethren and seeing one of the Egyptian's mistreating one of them. It angered him so much that he killed the man. I'm not sure whether or not the Egyptian woman that raised Moses as her son shared with him that she was not his real mom and that he really belonged to a Hebrew mother, but we can see just how Moses' life was full of uncertainties from that day forward after killing the Egyptian.

Moses had to flee from Pharaoh, the very man that helped raise him, into a strange land far away from that which he was familiar. Can you imagine the uncertainties, despair and darkness he felt in his heart from what surely had seemed to him, at that time, as some twist of fate? You see, God was in this plan concerning Moses' life more than what he could feel or see at that moment. I'm sure when Carlton was all grown up and was told by Doris that she was not his real mom and that his real mom "Shining Star" gave him up, he felt uncertainties, despair and darkness in his heart about why he was separated away from the rest of his sisters and brothers. By Carlton living away from his other siblings, he was as strange to them as they were to him. But just like Moses' life in the Bible, God had a plan for Carlton's life more than what he knew. As I said earlier, God's plan never looks like what we may have planned. Oftentimes, it does seem just the opposite of what we have in mind.

Remember that "gift" is the meaning of the name Doris, the lady who raised Carlton. Just by her name meaning gift, it is easily seen that God was in the midst of touching her heart to ask Carlton's real mom to take him home with her. She was a gift to Carlton and Carlton was a gift to her as well. He would need Doris, a saved and praying woman, more times than he would ever know.

Carlton shared his story with me about how Doris would many times keep him in church while traveling from place to place to various church services and great revivals. She would take him in the prayer lines so that he could be prayed over by many great men and women of God who were legends and who were sold out for the gospel. He said Doris would hold him on her knees and read the Bible out loud and explain it to him daily. She would speak life into him and pray without ceasing. She would mention often to him that someday he would be a preacher. And yes, today he is a preacher. That is why I now know that it is so important for parents to speak positive things into their children at a young age while they are growing so that when they are older, those positive words will help sustain them when disappointments come their way. And we know that in this life, many disappointments await us all.

Doris was a great evangelist that loved the Lord with all of her heart. She stayed on her face in prayer praying for the souls of the unsaved. God already knew that Carlton would need this praying woman of God in his life because there was much pain waiting up the road for both Doris and him. More than they knew. All of this was God's plan so that those good seeds could be planted in Carlton's heart to help prepare him for the roads of uncertainties that laid ahead that he was so unaware of.

Chapter 3: God's Protective Hands

Carlton shared with me how Doris was very protective of him. She would not let him go over to the neighbor's houses by himself unless she was with him. She would check on him in school to make sure he was doing his work and was not goofing off. At home, Doris would help him with his homework and if he wanted to go to any type of school games, she would take him herself. Now you know that young people, especially as they become teenagers, want to go to school games by themselves, but Doris wouldn't allow it. Carlton said that he didn't like that back then, but now when he looks over his life, he can see that it was God's protective hands working through Doris to help keep him from many dangers and temptations during his youth that could have caused him unnecessary pain. Isn't it amazing that when we are young, we can't see the many dangers lurking around the corners but our parents who have been living longer than we have, can see it all? Even in this, I can see how God was protecting Carlton for His use in His kingdom later on.

Earlier in the story about Moses, do you remember the uncertainties that came into Moses' life even though he was raised in one of the finest of homes: The King's Palace? Well it's the same here with Carlton. He was raised in a good and godly home, but life had its own twist of fate waiting along the way and just like Moses, Carlton's life had a lot of uncertainties.

As a young lad, Carlton had a mind to work and he started at the age of eleven doing little odd jobs to make money. One of the jobs that he had was assisting a man by the name of James Pruden with his food truck. This man loved the Lord as well and he kept Carlton encouraged in the things of God. Weekends in and weekends out, as he worked with Mr. Pruden, he could see how God's hands was on Mr. Pruden by the way he lived a godly life in front of him until his death. This was also God's plan for him to learn about the Lord as a young boy.

Chapter 4: The Move to New York City

As Carlton grew older, it wasn't long that Doris moved to New York City from Gates County where they were presently living. During the time that they were in New York City, Doris found work cleaning houses and Carlton found maintenance work at a daycare cleaning and buffing the floors and other things. Carlton was able to attend high school at Thomas Jefferson where he later graduated.

After living with her daughter for a while, Doris was able to find an apartment near the school where Carlton attended. After Carlton graduated from Thomas Jefferson High School, He continued to work at the daycare so that he could help Doris with whatever was needed at home. One night, while Doris was asleep and he was away at choir practice, someone slipped into their apartment and stole the TV. It was after this incident that Doris felt that it would be safer to move back to Gates County.

He shared that he and his mom would sit and talk about many things together and she would talk to him about life. She would talk about what to do to survive and how to avoid the negative paths that are always available to trap anyone who strayed. But as life would have it, in spite of the wise teaching that came from his mom, Carlton would stray onto many deadly paths that would change his life forever.

Chapter 5: Back Down South

After moving back down South to Gates County, Carlton met a young lady that he liked. When he told Doris about the young lady, Doris told him that the young lady was not the one for him. By then, Carlton's heart had fallen for her and he began to disobey what Doris told him. (You see, when a person's heart gets into a relationship, it is hard for that person to either think clearly or hear sound wisdom or instruction. Even when it is coming from the very person who raised them and knows what is best for them.) By Carlton still being a young man, the emotions in his heart for the young lady blinded him of what Doris saw concerning her and he chose to marry her. Carlton joined the military to make sure that he would have a stable income and insurance to take care of his family.

During his time in the military, things were going well. Eventually Carlton and his wife had two children, and this brought him much joy. Shortly after that, Carlton finished his four years in the Marines. He had the opportunity to see different parts of the world while being in the Marines and the money that he made allowed him to support his family like he desired. Life at this time seemed promising until one day, the tides turned. Carlton found his world turned upside down in a quick moment.

Before I tell the rest of his story, I want to talk to you about another young man written in the Bible by the name of Joseph. I want to share Joseph's story so that you can see that life happens and twist of fate can happen to any of us at any time. These tragic times were going on with many men and women even in the Bible days.

Chapter 6: Life Happens

In the book of Genesis, starting in the 37th chapter, there was a young boy named Joseph. Joseph was born in his father's old age and because of this, his father loved him more than his other sons. This love that his father had for him made his brothers hate him with a deadly passion. One day his father made him a beautiful colorful coat, and this angered his brothers even more. When Joseph's brothers saw the favoritism that their father had toward Joseph over them, they hated Joseph to the point where they could not even speak a kind word to him.

As time would have it, one day Joseph's father sent him to check on his brothers who were working the fields. When Joseph's brothers looked and saw him afar off coming towards them, hate rose in their heart and they plotted to bring harm to him. As the story goes on, when Joseph came to his brothers, they stripped him of the decorative robe he was wearing, and they took him and threw him into the waterless cistern. After that, they sat down to eat their meals as if nothing had happened. Suddenly, they looked up and saw a caravan of Ishmaelites coming from Gilead with camels loaded with spices, balm and myrrh. They were on their way down to Egypt. Joseph's brothers saw this as an opportunity to sell Joseph to the travelers hoping that he would not be seen any more. They killed a goat and soaked Joseph's colorful coat in the goat's blood. They hoped that this would confirm their lie that he was killed by some wild animal and the only thing that they found of him was his destroyed coat.

As the story goes, Joseph's father did believe their lie about his son and mourned for him many days. But as you continue to read the story, Joseph was alive and well. After reaching Egypt, the Ishmaelites sold him to Potiphar, one of Pharaoh's officials, the captain of the guard. In spite of all the wrong that was done to Joseph, he eventually found favor with Potiphar and was given authority over everything that belonged to him, except his wife. As you continue reading the story, you will see how "fate took a twist" in Joseph's life once again. *Genesis 37:1-36 (NIV)*

Chapter 7: Twist of Fate

Back in the 37th chapter of Genesis, it was bad enough that Joseph's own brothers hated him out of jealousy and had him sold off to strange men who then took him into a strange country. But the nerve of having to lie to their old aged father saying that Joseph, their baby brother was dead. Now, according to Genesis 39, things were about to stir up for poor Joseph yet again.

As the story goes, Joseph was very strong and attractive, and this caught the eye of Potiphar's wife. She was so attracted to Joseph that she would catch him alone day after day after day begging him to sleep with her. Joseph was a godly man and because he loved and respected his boss, he would brush Potiphar's wife words off by saying "No. I will not do this wicked and disrespectful thing to God". Well of course, this did not sit well with Potiphar's wife. So, one day as she came begging him to sleep with her once again and hearing him say no again, she grabbed him, and Joseph ran off for his life leaving his cloak behind.

After seeing what had just happened and seeing the cloak left in her hands, Potiphar's wife saw this as an opportunity to get back at Joseph. She began to cry out for help saying that joseph had tried to make sport of her. Of course, when her husband heard of this, he burned with anger and had Joseph thrown into prison. But as you continue to read the story, it says that God was even with Joseph in the prison. He found favor with the warden and the warden gave him authority over all of the prisoners and the prison. *Genesis 39:1-2 (NIV)*

Chapter 8: A Word of Encouragement

I have just finished sharing two awesome stories with you from the Bible. Both Moses' and Joseph's lives started out well. Moses was found by Pharaoh's daughter and raised in the king's palace. Joseph was born in his father's old age which caused his father to have an overwhelming love and favor for him. Both men thought they had it made until one day life or some twist of fate happened. You see, this is how life is. We can see narrowly down the path of life, but we can't see around the bends that life's road has. Therefore, we are often caught off guard with whatever may be around the bend. As you see from the two stories, the mighty hand of a power higher than us, which is God, always sees ahead. And yes, He always has a plan.

According to *Proverbs 16:9 (NIV),* it says: *"In their hearts humans plan their course, but the Lord establishes their steps."* Many times, in life, just like Moses and Joseph, we can have many plans of our own and they can be good plans but oftentimes they just don't work out like we had hoped. I chose these two stories to talk about to allow you to fully get an understanding about the story in the next chapter.

This story is about a man I have come to know who was willing to share his life's story with me. This man, named Carlton, had plans about many things concerning his life but guess what? Life happens. Oh yes, life itself has many twists of fate awaiting around the bend for us all. May this story encourage you to see that we all have a story or two and the people in the Bible were not excluded. Hopefully, by the time you finish hearing about Carlton's story, you will take hope in knowing that you are not alone and as humans, we all have many bridges over troubled waters to cross. We all have to endure many things at times that are not our fault but yet we have to pay the price of shame and pain for it. However, in the end, we do win again and again.

Chapter 9: The Day the Sun Stopped Shining

Carlton had finished his course in the military and was now living at home in Gates County. It was a fine summer day and he was outside mowing his yard. This day was, from what he could see, no different from any of his other days. Whenever he had a day off from work, he did whatever he could around the house. His family had gone shopping, and all felt well. Suddenly, his life of peace and freedom was about to be disrupted in a horrific way more that he could have ever fathomed.

As Carlton continued to mow his grass, he noticed that a car was driving into his yard. He knew the man, so he went to see what he wanted only to hear the man say to him, "Your daddy is coming to see you". Carlton said he thought nothing more of it but told the guy "Ok." He thought that the guy was talking about his stepdad coming to see him. The guy left and Carlton went back to mowing his grass when suddenly he heard another car coming into his driveway. Turning to see who it was, to his surprise, it was a Sheriff's car. He walks over to the car to see what the Sheriff wanted only to hear the Sheriff say "Just get in the car. We need to take you to the police station because we received a phone call that you have done some wrong acts." Needless to say, for Carlton the sun stopped shining in his life that day. Carlton said he knew that he had not done anything wrong but because it was the Sheriff, he felt that he had better obey the sheriff and find out what was going on. He described to me that while he was in the car, the Sheriff pointed a gun at his head and said, "I ought to kill you right now for what you have done". Carlton said he kept asking the policeman, "What have I done?" The policeman just kept on saying to him "You know what you did?"

From there Carlton was taken to jail until his trial date. He said none of the accusers showed up in court and that did not surprise him because he had not done anything. As Carlton told me his story, he said that if he knew the law like he knows it now, he would have never gotten into the police car without a warrant nor would he had signed any papers while in the courthouse. It is so sad when you think of the millions of people who do not know the law and have signed papers thinking that the papers were in their favor only to find out later that they weren't. From being in his own yard mowing the grass on a sun shiny day, he was suddenly hauled away straight to the courthouse like a criminal and in a short time after that he was sentenced to many years in prison for something that he never did. It was in this season of darkness he cried out to God, "Why?"

Chapter 10: God Why?

While Carlton was in prison, his heart was broken into millions of pieces as he tried hard to get his thoughts together of why all of this had happened to him. "Why?", is the question that has fallen on many of our lips many times when horrific things happen unexpectedly in our lives. Remember the stories about Moses and Joseph and the twists of fate that fell upon their lives when they least expected it? Carlton described to me the many days that he cried and cried while lying on his bunk in prison. He would ask God the questions, "Why me? What did I do to deserve this?" As time went on, God began to comfort him in many ways allowing him to know that he is a God of His word. That He will never leave us nor forsake us *Hebrew 13:5 (NIV),* no matter how long it takes or no matter how hard it gets. The awesome thing about God is that He is omniscient meaning that He is all knowing and all seeing. Nothing is ever shocking to God. He is the God of the past, present and future. Even when things happen in our lives and we may not understand it all in the beginning, slowly by and by, we will. Yes, in time we will understand it all.

Chapter 11: Favor behind the Prison Walls

Do you remember in the book of Genesis, Chapter 39, when Potiphar's wife's false accusations caused Joseph to be thrown into prison, but while he was there God gave him favor with the warden and the warden gave him authority over the prison? Well, this is what happen with Carlton. While being in prison with false accusations, God gave Carlton favor with many of the inmates as well as with the warden. The warden gave him the keys to the library and allowed him to have church in there with the inmates. The inmates loved him so much that they would iron his clothes for him and protect him from any other inmates who may have tried to hurt him. Wow. While I listened to Carlton tell me about his life in prison, it touched my heart just to see how faithful God is to His people no matter where they may be.

Many times, while in prison, Carlton would pray for the inmates who came to him for prayers. Many inmates were saved, set free and delivered as the power of God would show up behind the jail cells among them as they prayed. Carlton shared with me that he prayed for many of the inmates to be released out of prison and he saw many of them leave. But even though he was overjoyed to see the inmates' prayers answered, he would begin to ask God, "Lord when will my time come for me to be released?" He said the

Lord allow him to know that when he was ready again for society, he would be released. You see, God already knew that by Carlton being set up and falsely accused in such an unjust way, there was much anger, unforgiveness and shame built up on the inside of him and being released too soon could have caused harm to himself or to his accusers.

One night while Carlton was sleeping, he was awakened with tears running down his face and he was speaking in tongues (heavenly language). Praise God. God had filled him with the holy ghost in his sleep. Just hearing this testimony shook my very soul because this lets me see just how great our God is. He shared that one day while he was in the prison shower he blanked out and he felt himself sliding down the shower wall. When he opened his eyes there was a white foggy cloud in front of him and God spoke to him saying, "This is how fast life can end. Get your house in order". He said from that day forward he knew to get totally in tune with God and not to be straddling the fence in any area.

Many times, while walking the prison yard, Carlton would pretend that he was still in the military. He said the military teachings and trainings that he had learned while being in the Marines helped sustain him through many lonely days, nights and years. He honestly feels now that if it wasn't for the hard training that he had endured while in the Marines, he may not have had the strength to make it in prison. Especially, seeing so much wicked, sinful and deadly things being done behind bars.

Isn't it amazing that even though the desire was in his heart to join the Marines so that he could have good benefits for his family, we can now see that the four years of training in the military really prepared him for the unseen suffering that he had to go through later in his life. Hearing stories like this allows us to see how much God is in charge of our lives. When we think the planning that we do is all about us, we find out later that God's loving hands were in it all the time, making sure that we get on the right path that will help us to be better equipped for our future endeavors in life. *Proverbs 16:9 (NIV)* says: *"In their hearts humans plan their course, but the Lord establishes their steps." Psalm 32:8 (NIV)* says: *"I will instruct you and teach you in the way you should go; I will counsel you with my loving eye on you."* So, as we see here, it's ok to plan but be willing to accept God's best plan for your life when he steps in and changes them which is always for His glory.

Chapter 12: Released from Prison to Home

Many years had come and gone while Carlton was still behind bars. Through it all, God had proved himself faithful to him over and over again. Finally, the day came when Carlton was given those faithful words that he had been waiting so patiently to hear from the warden: "You can now go home". Upon hearing the news that he could now go home; he shared his excitement but also his fears. He was excited that he was finally freed to go and to do as he pleased once again without being watched over or without being told what to do. However, he was afraid of what the world now had to offer a branded person such as himself. He said he told the Lord, with the lies that have been told on him causing this foul reputation to be now attached to his name, no one will want to marry him or will want to have anything to do with him ever again. He told the Lord, "I guess I will just have to stay single for the rest of my days and serve you." But as I said from the beginning, life has a way of throwing us curve balls that we often times do not see coming. Likewise, life often has showers of blessings too, that we may not be able to see at the moment.

After getting out of prison, Carlton stayed with his stepfather. His loving aunt, who raised him, had now gone on to be with the Lord. He still talks about her even to this day of how such a good woman she was and how much he misses her dearly.

After getting out of prison, God favored Carlton to be able to continue working with the same man that he worked with while in prison. In prison there is something that is called a work release where the inmates can work outside of the prison during the day and then return back to the prison at night. Carlton was one who was favored by the hands of God to qualify for the work release program. So being free now, he was trying to find his way back to feeling good about himself and about life.

As time went on, a young lady showed interest in him. Since he had been away for such a long, long time, it felt nice to have a lady to be interested in him knowing that he had a prison record. Eventually, Carlton married the young lady, which was now his second wife. To this marriage, two children were born. Remember back in the early part of his story when Carlton was taken away to prison from his first wife and two children? While he was in prison, his first wife divorced him. A lot to lose for something that he had not done. Do you remember when I shared about how when you think all is well, out of nowhere that old twist of fate sticks its ugly head up? This is what happened. Things went down south and the second marriage was short lived. Even though Doris raised him well by keeping him in church and in the company of positive people, as he grew older, he chose different paths himself that led him into much troubled waters.

Chapter 13: More Winding Roads

As one can see, from the time that Carlton was born and given away by his mom to his mom's sister to raise him, there have been many winding roads that he had to travel. But through every step that he had to take; we can see that the favor of God was on his life. By Carlton having a prison record, he didn't think that he would ever get a very good paying job with benefits, but he did. God allowed a very precious man by the name of Mr. Willie, who was working at Wal-Mart at that time, to put in a good word for him. He got the job and has been working there now for twenty-five years.

From the first day hat he started working at Wal-Mart, Carlton found favor on every hand and people just loved him. Wal-Mart has become a ministry for him. Workers, as well as the customers, often stop and share their problems with him. He shared that before being hired at Wal-Mart, he had put in applications for two jobs. One was the Shipyard and the other one was Wal-Mart. What do you know? Both jobs called him on the same day, and he chose to respond to Wal-Mart. This story is about to get interesting because this is where I first met Carlton.

Chapter 14: Divine Destiny

I am proud to say that this man whom I met so long ago and this man who shared his life story with me is now my husband. Oh yes, I am Christine White the wife of this mysterious man. Let me tell you how I came to meet this guy.

I had been working at Wal-Mart for a year and then I left to try working somewhere else. This other job did not work out for me, so I returned to Wal-Mart and was hired back. The second time I was hired back to Wal-Mart, it wasn't long before Carlton got hired. I will never forget that day. I was also working at Askewville's School as a bus driver. When I would get off of the evening bus route, I would head to Wal-Mart to work the evening shift.

One day as I arrived at Wal-Mart, I came through the front door walking fast trying to get to the time clock. I remember as I walked through the front door, I saw a new guy working on the door as the greeter, but I didn't think anything of him. He was just another new worker to me. I was a cashier so after clocking in at the back of the store, I headed toward the front of the store to my workstation that I was assigned to and started my evening shift. Every day I would show up to work and would watch Carlton stand quietly at the door greeting the people as they would come in. It wasn't long that the boss moved him from being a greeter to bringing in the shopping carts as well as to do maintenance work. He was very good at what he did, and I noticed that he worked faithfully from the heart. I found out that he was a preacher and I would talk to him a little about my life and the many winding roads and twists of fate that had occurred in my life.

As time went on, I found out that he was so easy to talk to and it became hard for me to stop thinking about him even after I got off work. What intrigued me about this guy was the fact that he would remember my conversations. For a man to remember a lady's conversations, even after she has gone away out of his presence, was a big plus for me.

And one day when he was working, I asked him did he want a piece of candy and he said yes. But instead of me reaching into my pocket to give him the candy, I turned my pocket towards him and let him reach his hands into my pocket to get the candy himself (lol). I would often tease him about that day by saying that I had some love portion on that candy, and this is how I won his heart. But clearly you can see, it was God's hand of guidance that led us into each other's lives. I like to think that it was ***divine destiny***. I believe that ***divine destiny*** is sent from the heart of God to bring glory to His name and to bring joy and fulfillment to His children whom he loves deeply and yearns for them to be happy.

As we continued to frequently conversate, I felt that I really liked this guy and I wrote him a letter. To be honest, after I wrote him the letter and shared my life story with him by telling him that I was separated from my first husband and have four children, I did not expect to hear from him. So, when he responded to the letter, I was shocked that he wanted someone like me. But as you can see, God has a plan for our lives even when we don't see the how, the when, or the where. God cares about our needs, wants and yes, our heart's desires.

Eventually, I brought Carlton over and introduced him to my children. I wanted my children to meet him and for him to meet them because it was a package deal. I wanted Carlton to know that if he loved me, He would have to love my children as well. I can truly say that from day one that Carlton started dating me, he started giving into my life and towards my children even before we got married. He showed me that he was willing to take me and the children as his own. In the year of 1998, we were married and are still going strong. I worked at Wal-Mart with this precious man for thirteen years before moving on to do something else. Yes, God is faithful and true to his children.

Chapter 15: The Power to Forgive

After working at Wal-Mart for a while, one day Carlton received a phone call. Not knowing who it was, he came to the phone and said, "This is Carlton, how may I help you?" To his surprise, it was the guy who had framed him. It was the one who had lied on him and had caused him to serve years in prison. He said that he could not believe that this was happening. This guy was on the other end of the phone asking him for forgiveness for lying on him and causing him to serve time. The guy told him that he would call the rest of Carlton's family and tell them that it was him (the accuser) all along who had falsely accused Carlton.

Carlton shared with me that he told the guy that he forgives him. Carlton knew that God had changed his heart and that even though he could not get the years back for what was done to him, he trusts that God would reward him by and by for doing the right things toward people in spite of what they may do or have done to him. He understood the power of forgiveness.

Epilogue

Carlton Matthew White, Sr. is an anointed writer. I noticed after we were married that he loves to write letters. He writes to whoever God drops in his heart. He doesn't even have to know the person well, but as the Lord leads him, he will write and encourage them. Many people have shared their testimony of how much Carlton's letters have blessed their lives and has given them hope in dark times.

Carlton is also an anointed song writer and sings under the anointing of God. Many can bear witness that his songs have brought much joy, peace and happiness into their lives. He has recorded seven CDs, and more is to come. With his love for God, people and music, I know there is no stopping this man from sharing his life to a hurting world through these gifts.

Carlton is also a preacher and a teacher of the gospel. He has never gone to seminary or anything like that, but you will often hear him say, in his own words,

"With the things that I have gone through in my life, my life experiences and by the grace of God, this qualifies me to preach the good news to all men allowing them to see that God is real and he is well able to heal, set free and deliver any man, woman, boy

or girl who needs to be healed and delivered from the dark twists of fate that awaits them down the winding roads of life. No matter what you may be going through, it's only a temporary inconvenience for a permanent improvement in your life. The safest place in the whole wide world is in the will of God."

This man, Carlton Matthew White, Sr., who I met years ago, is the love of my life. A dear friend to the end. This book **"A Man Like Moses Walking in the Path of Joseph"** was written to encourage all people that if God can do it for Moses, Joseph and for Carlton, he can do it for you. No matter how dark twists of fate try to hinder our lives, with the power of God Almighty on our side, we do win in every situation every time. And yes, we do succeed.

Carlton and Christine White are the Pastors of *"A Practical Way of Living Evangelistic Ministry of Deliverance"* where they teach and preach the gospel worldwide through live streaming. Carlton gives all honor to Jesus Christ, his Saviour and Lord, and special thanks to Christine Swain White, his wife who helped to make this book, **"A Man like Moses Walking in the Path of Joseph",** possible for him.

www.ingramcontent.com/pod-product-compliance
Lightning Source LLC
LaVergne TN
LVHW041459070426
835507LV00009B/702